Enuma Elish

(The Original Text, With Brief Commentary)

Ken Goudsward

ISBN 978-1-989940-39-6

2021 Creative Commons Attribution-ShareAlike 4.0 Intl.

Dimensionfold Publishing

Table Of Contents

Introduction 1

Cast of Characters 2

Tablet I 3

Tablet II 16

Tablet III 24

Tablet IV 29

Tablet V 38

Tablet VI 51

Tablet VII 64

Narrative Summary 73

Conclusion 76

Introduction

The Enuma Elish is often referred to as *The Seven Tablets of Creation* or "the Mesopotamian creation myth". While these titles are not entirely inappropriate, they tend to put a specific slant on preconceptions of what the story truly is. This is not a myth. There are no gods involved. The main characters are ordinary people, though not necessarily human ones. There are politicians and businessmen and housewives. There are people with relatable skills, dreams, and plans, some of which become thwarted.

The title "Enuma Elish" is derived from the opening lines of the piece, "When on High", a fact that is rather strange considering that this is not the actual translation in English. The English translation used here comes from *Mesopotamian Creation Stories* by W.G. Lambert and is used under Creative Commons license. It has been lightly edited in this edition. Whatever small translation discrepancies may or may not be inherent in the translation seem to become nearly a moot point, when one realizes the true nature of the story. It becomes very hard to ignore once you see the pattern, regardless of the words used, for the concepts themselves are so overwhelmingly glaring.

Although the opening verses do appear to read like a typical "creation myth" the reader will soon see that this story is not about the creation of the universe at all, at least not in a traditional sense.

Cast of Characters

Apsu and Tiamat – the "first gods"
Lahmu and Lahamu – second generation gods
Ansar and Kisar
Anu – son of Ansar
Ea and Nudimmud – sons of Anu
Damkina – Ea's wife
Marduk (aka. Bel) – son of Ea and Damkina
Mummu – Apsu's advisor
Hubur - Mother who forms everything
Quingu and the 11 Anunnaki
The Igigi – the court and council
Kaka – Ansar's visier
Nibiru – the crossing of the ecliptic and the Milky Way
Nannar (aka. Sin) – the moon
Shamash – the sun
Usmu – Visier of Marduk's new kingdom
Lullu – a new race of man devised by Marduk

Tablet I

1 When the heavens above did not exist,
2 And earth beneath had not come into being —
3 There was Apsu, the first in order, their begetter,
4 And Tiamat the artisan who gave birth to them all;
5 They had mingled their waters together
6 Before meadows had coalesced and swamps were to be found —
7 When not one of the gods had been formed
8 Or had come into being, when no destinies had been decreed

The first section ostensibly summarizes a primordial state before creation. Two divine entities Apsu and Tiamat conceived of a plan for creation.

The next section introduces a number of minor characters, seemingly in several generations. These are said to have been created by Apsu and Tiamat, although it is not clear whether these two created the rest directly, or if a series of normal sexual reproduction took place to produce the generations. The latter case is most likely, obviously, and appears to fit a genealogical recreation as outlined in the introduction. This supposition will be born out later in the text, as certain characters are identified by relationship.

9 The gods were created within them:
10 Lahmu and Lahamu were formed and came into being.
11 While they grew and increased in stature
12 Ansar and Kisar, who excelled them, were created.
13 They prolonged their days, they multiplied their years.

14 Anu, their son, could rival his fathers.
15 Anu, the son, equalled Ansar,

    Lines 11 to 15 speak of the success of these early characters. They enjoyed longevity and became powerful. Line 16 speaks more clearly of yet another generation, this one begat by Anu. His son Nudimmud rose to prominence as a strong and intelligent man.

16 And Anu begat Nudimmud, his own equal.
17 Nudimmud was the champion among his fathers:
18 Profoundly discerning, wise, of robust strength;
19 Very much stronger than his father's begetter, Ansar
20 He had no rival among the gods, his brothers.

21 The divine brothers came together,
22 Their made much noise, upsetting Tiamat
23 They jarred the nerves of Tiamat,
24 Their dancing spread alarm in Anduruna.
25 Apsu did not diminish their clamour,
26 And Tiamat was silent when confronted with them.
27 Their conduct was displeasing to her,
28 Yet though their behaviour was not good, she wished to spare them.

    The primeval two, Apsu and Tiamat are concerned by the new generation. Tiamat is particularly troubled, but Apsu does not deem to dole out retribution. Tiamat seems to smoulder in silent rage and scheming, though she wishes to punish, but not destroy, her children.

29 Thereupon Apsu, the begetter of the great gods,
30 Called Mummu, his vizier, and addressed him,
31 "Vizier Mummu, who gratifies my pleasure,
32 Come, let us go to Tiamat!"
33 They went and sat, facing Tiamat,
34 As they conferred about the gods, their sons.
35 Apsu opened his mouth
36 And addressed Tiamat
37 "Their behaviour has become displeasing to me
38 And I cannot rest in the day-time or sleep at night.
39 I will destroy and break up their way of life
40 That silence may reign and we may sleep."
41 When Tiamat heard this
42 She raged and cried out to her spouse,
43 She cried in distress, fuming within herself,
44 She grieved over the evil,
45 "How can we destroy what we have given birth to?
46 Though their behaviour causes distress, let us tighten discipline graciously."
47 Mummu spoke up with counsel for Apsu—
48 (As from) a rebellious vizier was the counsel of his Mummu—
49 "My lord, destroy, that lawless way of life,
50 That you may rest in the day-time and sleep by night!"
51 Apsu was pleased with him, his face beamed
52 Because he had plotted evil against the gods, his sons.
53 Mummu put his arms around Apsu's neck,
54 He sat on his knees kissing him.

After consulting his advisor, Apsu decides that indeed, the children must be destroyed. Tiamat attempts to dissuade him, arguing for a more reasonable punishment, but Apsu's mind is already made up.

We are now introduced to a new character, Ea. Ea is one of the younger generation. He is probably the great-great-grandson of Apsu. Somehow, he finds out about Apsu's decision, and immediately begins to plan a counterattack against Apsu.

55 What they plotted in their gathering
56 Was reported to the gods, their sons.
57 The gods heard it and were frantic.
58 They were overcome with silence and sat quietly.
59 Ea, who excels in knowledge, the skilled and learned,
60 Ea, who knows everything, perceived their tricks.
61 He fashioned it and made it to be all-embracing,
62 He executed it skilfully as supreme—his pure incantation.
63 He recited it and set it on the waters,
64 He poured sleep upon him as he was slumbering deeply.
65 He put Apsu to slumber as he poured out sleep,
66 And Mummu, the counsellor, was breathless with agitation.
67 He split (Apsu's) sinews, ripped off his crown,
68 Carried away his aura and put it on himself.
69 He bound Apsu and killed him;
70 Mummu he confined and handled roughly.
71 He set his dwelling upon Apsu,
72 And laid hold on Mummu, keeping the nose-rope in his hand.

Ea prepares a poison which he administers to Apsu in his sleep. Ea takes Apsu's advisor prisoner, and kills Apsu, stealing his crown and garments.

73 After Ea had bound and slain his enemies,
74 Had achieved victory over his foes,
75 He rested quietly in his chamber,
76 He called it Apsu, whose shrines he appointed.
77 Then he founded his living-quarters within it,
78 And Ea and Damkina, his wife, sat in splendour.
79 In the chamber of the destinies, the room of the archetypes.

It seems both intriguing and perhaps a bit disconcerting that the word Apsu now comes to be used as the name of a place rather than of a person. If this is the case here, what are we to make of some of the other names mentioned briefly. Might some of these also be references for places rather than specific characters? They might actually refer to other lands or countries, or planets. This fits with a general trend in ancient middle eastern literature. The descendants of a great hero are often referred to by the original hero's name. This pattern is well-documented in the Bible for example, where Israel is originally the name of one specific man, then later it is the name of all his descendants, and eventually becomes the name of their land. This is perhaps the most well-known case, but it is by no means an isolated incident.

Thus, a second reading of lines 10 to 22 is recommended in view of this trend, with an openness to the possibility that all these tangential names are in fact the names of other societies or civilizations, possibly spread across the earth or possibly even on other planets. I suggest that this interpretation fits the text better than an assumption that the names refer to specific people. For *"Lahmu and Lahamu were formed and came into being."* And *"While they increased in stature, Ansar and Kisar, who excelled them, were created."* The verbiage used is very apt to describe the formation and progress of civilizations. Likewise, for Anu and his "son" Nudimmud. This reading also provides realism to the otherwise unbelievable claims of longevity that we see both here and in such other texts as the Sumerian King Lists and the Biblical book of Genesis.

It must be noted that the concept civilizations elsewhere can be interpreted in a wide variety of ways. These places may simply be neighboring tribes, cities or countries. However, such interpretations may be thinking too small. The text thus far has given no indication of life on other planets, or of space travel between them. It is only mentioned at this point, in case the reader is already familiar with such theories as proposed by Zechariah Sitchin[1] and others. This idea will be examined further as the text progresses. It must be acknowledged as well that the theory appears to be supported by a vast body of evidence and partially buried clues within the Sumerian literature, and within the Hebrew literature as well, as discussed in my book *UFOs In The Bible*.[2]

All speculation aside for now, it seems that Ea moves into Apsu's palace with his wife, and here they

---

[1] Sitchin, Zechariah; *The 12th Planet*, 1976, Stein and Day, ISBN 0-8128-1939-X
[2] Goudsward, Ken; *UFOs In The Bible*, 2021, Dimensionfold Publishing, ISBN 978-1-989940-08-2

conceive a child who would go by two names, Bel and Marduk. Interestingly, this place is referred to as the "chamber of the destinies," and the "room of the archetypes."

80 The wisest of the wise, the sage of the gods, Bel was conceived.
81 In Apsu was Marduk born,
82 In pure Apsu was Marduk born.
83 Ea his father begat him,
84 Damkina his mother bore him.
85 He sucked the breasts of goddesses,
86 A nurse reared him and filled him with terror.
87 His figure was well developed, the glance of his eyes was dazzling,
88 His growth was manly, he was mighty from the beginning.
89 Anu, his father's begetter, saw him,
90 He exulted and smiled; his heart filled with joy.
91 Anu rendered him perfect: his divinity was remarkable,
92 And he became very lofty, excelling them in his attributes.
93 His members were incomprehensibly wonderful,
94 Incapable of being grasped with the mind, hard even to look on.
95 Four were his eyes, four his ears,
96 Flame shot forth as he moved his lips.
97 His four ears grew large,
93 And his eyes likewise took in everything.
99 His figure was lofty and superior in comparison with the gods,
100 His limbs were surpassing, his nature was superior.
101 'Mari-utu, Mari-utu,

102 The Son, the Sun-god, the Sun-god of the gods.'
103 He was clothed with the aura of the Ten Gods, so exalted was his strength,

The description of Marduk given here is very strange. He may have been a two-headed giant. This may coincide with other ancient mythologies of the region, particularly those of the Nephilim, and the "mighty men of old". This may explain the tangential dead-ended reference to Nudimmud, son of Anu in line 16 to 20. It may be that both of Anu's sons were giants. In any case, Anu is impressed enough with his grandson Marduk, that he creates several custom-made weapons as a gift for him.

Perhaps a simpler interpretation is that Marduk was a colony that achieved independence and created a more advanced technological civilization. Bear this in mind while reading the remainder of Tablet I, for it seems to speak of numerous nations, factions, corporations, and alliances all vying for dominance and engaged in a technological arms race.

104 The Fifty Dreads were loaded upon him.
105 Anu formed and gave birth to the four winds,
106 He delivered them to him, "My son, let them whirl!"
107 He formed dust and set a hurricane to drive it,
108 He made a wave to bring consternation on Tiamat.
109 Tiamat was confounded; day and night she was frantic.
110 The gods took no rest, they . . . .
111 In their minds they plotted evil,
112 And addressed their mother Tiamat,

113 "When Apsu, your spouse, was killed,
114 You did not go at his side, but sat quietly.
115 The four dreadful winds have been fashioned
116 To throw you into confusion, and we cannot sleep.
117 You gave no thought to Apsu, your spouse,
113 Nor to Mummu, who is a prisoner. Now you sit alone.
119 Henceforth you will be in frantic consternation!
120 And as for us, who cannot rest, you do not love us!
121 Consider our burden, our eyes are hollow.
122 Break the immovable yoke that we may sleep.
123 Make battle, avenge them!
124 [...] reduce to nothingness!
125 Tiamat heard, the speech pleased her,
126 She said, "Let us make demons, as you have advised."
127 The gods assembled within her.
128 They conceived [...] against the gods their begetters.
129 They [...] and took the side of Tiamat,
130 Fiercely plotting, unresting by night and day,
131 Lusting for battle, raging, storming,
132 They set up a host to bring about conflict.

The narrative suddenly shifts here from Tiamat to a new character named Hubur.

133 Mother Hubur, who forms everything,
134 Supplied irresistible weapons, and gave birth to giant serpents.
135 They had sharp teeth, they were merciless . . . .
136 With poison instead of blood she filled their bodies.
137 She clothed the fearful monsters with dread,
138 She loaded them with an aura and made them godlike.

139 She said, "Let their onlooker feebly perish,
140 May they constantly leap forward and never retire."
141 She created the Hydra, the Dragon, the Hairy Hero
142 The Great Demon, the Savage Dog, and the Scorpion-man,
143 Fierce demons, the Fish-man, and the Bull-man,
144 Carriers of merciless weapons, fearless in the face of battle.
145 Her commands were tremendous, not to be resisted.
146 Altogether she made eleven of that kind.
147 Among the gods, her sons, whom she constituted her host,
148 She exalted Qingu, and magnified him among them.
149 The leadership of the army, the direction of the host,
150 The bearing of weapons, campaigning, the mobilization of conflict,
151 The chief executive power of battle, supreme command,
152 She entrusted to him and set him on a throne,
153 "I have cast the spell for you and exalted you in the host of the gods,
154 I have delivered to you the rule of all the gods.
155 You are indeed exalted, my spouse, you are renowned,
156 Let your commands prevail over all the Anunnaki."
157 She gave him the Tablet of Destinies and fastened it to his breast,
158 "Your order may not be changed; let the utterance of your mouth be firm."
159 After Qingu was elevated and had acquired the power of Anuship,
160 He decreed the destinies for the gods, her sons:
161 "May the utterance of your mouths subdue the fire-

god,
162 May your poison by its accumulation put down aggression."

There appears to be a correlation in lines 141 to 148 with the signs of the zodiac.[3] Several of the "creations of Hubur" appear as obviously recognizable parallels to the zodiacal signs still in use today. Scorpio, Aquarius, and Taurus are easily spotted in the names of the Scorpion-man, the Fish-man, and the Bull-man. Some of the other others are more subtle, but they number eleven, and with the explicit addition of Qingu their number becomes twelve. The problem with this idea is that the order of the signs listed by Hubur does not match the order of the recognizable signs in our zodiac. Keep this in mind, as it will be addressed later.

Hubur, the "creator" of these twelve is a common word in Sumerian, meaning "river". A somewhat banal interpretation of this section might be that twelve cities were founded along the banks of a great river. In many ways a river does create cities, and this is especially true in arid landscapes such as the middle east, as is clearly demonstrated by a quick example of the Nile river in Egypt.

I postulate a more cosmic interpretation. The twelve zodiac signs are and always have been a way to partition the sky into manageable segments. To say that Mars is "in Aries" or "in Gemini" simply means that one might find its current location by referring to readily recognizable

---

[3] Note that the word 'zodiac' itself does not appear in the Mesopotamian texts, but is of much later Greek origin, and means "cycle of the animals"

patterns of stars in order to determine what generally area to attempt a Martian observation.

In this framework, the allusion to a "river" is a reference to the Milky Way galaxy, which does appear to cut across the sky much as a river cuts across the land. The ancient Mesopotamians had a very good understanding of cosmic topography. They knew that the earth was a small marble amidst a vast expanse. Their understanding of the relative motions of planets and other cosmic bodies set against a backdrop of distant stars enabled them to track and predict the seasons as well as eclipses and other relevant phenomenon to a degree of accuracy that today requires powerful computer algorithms.

Thus, this river of the galactic disk was seen as the source of all life. Life migrated out from the galactic core, into the outer reaches of the galaxy, including the spiral arm that includes our own sun and the solar system that we call home.

We tend to be so home focussed that we forget that we are but a baby planet on a backwater arm of a humdrum galaxy. Not so, the ancients. They somehow grasped this concept. They knew the importance of tying our location to a greater conceptualization. This is why the zodiacal signs were worth bothering with. Each of these constellation points us in a different direction. By observing the stars we look "out there" and realize that perhaps we are not alone. By tying this behaviour to a fixed local directionality we achieve a means of thinking about direction in three dimensions. "Out there" becomes narrowed to "over here". This allows planetary visitors to communicate in rough terms about where they have been or where they are going.

This is the context in which the Anunnaki are suddenly introduced. However, in my opinion, the Anunnaki are not gods or even personal entities at all. Anunnaki seems to be a collective term for these directions, these twelve segments of sky arc. This should really be no surprise, for the word Anunnaki is universally accepted among scholars to be a combination of the words "An" meaning 'sky', and 'ki' indicating the earth. Hence, the Anunnaki, is simply the "earth-sky" or the view of the sky from the vantage point of earth.

Thus, we can now glean some sense from such statements as *"the direction of the host, The bearing of weapons, [...] the mobilization of conflict,"* as exactly what they sound like. They are literally references to the direction and orientation of a continuing battle in three-dimensional space surrounding the earth. Additionally, when we read of a mysterious Tablet of Destinies, it makes sense to interpret this in an algorithmic light. Good algorithms plus accurate data results in accurate predictive modelling. When Quingu is set upon a throne and given chief executive power of battle, he is most likely being given computer access. When the "spell is cast for him" he is given the correct algorithmic programs to run and the accurate dataset to run through them. To me, this makes a lot more sense that interpreting such objects as simply magical spells.

Tablet II

1 Tiamat gathered together her creation
2 And organised battle against the gods, her offspring.
3 Henceforth Tiamat plotted evil because of Apsu
4 It became known to Ea that she had arranged the conflict.
5 Ea heard this matter,
6 He lapsed into silence in his chamber and sat motionless.
7 After he had reflected and his anger had subsided
8 He directed his steps to Ansar his father.
9 He entered the presence of the father of his begetter, Ansar,
10 And related to him all of Tiamat's plotting.
11 "My father, Tiamat our mother has conceived a hatred for us,
12 She has established a host in her savage fury.
13 All the gods have turned to her,
14 Even those you begat also take her side
15 They […] and took the side of Tiamat,
16 Fiercely plotting, unresting by night and day,
17 Lusting for battle, raging, storming,
18 They set up a host to bring about conflict.

This next section is a repetition of lines 133 to 162 of Tablet I. This may indicate that Tablet II was a later work quoting the original. Or it may be repeated to stress the importance of the specific passage which outlines the zodiacal partitioning and Qingu's "computer".

19 Mother Hubur, who forms everything,
20 Supplied irresistible weapons, and gave birth to giant serpents.
21 They had sharp teeth, they were merciless.
22 With poison instead of blood she filled their bodies.
23 She clothed the fearful monsters with dread,
24 She loaded them with an aura and made them godlike.
25 (She said,) "Let their onlooker feebly perish,
26 May they constantly leap forward and never retire."
27 She created the Hydra, the Dragon, the Hairy Hero,
28 The Great Demon, the Savage Dog, and the Scorpion-man,
29 Fierce demons, the Fish-man, and the Bull-man,
30 Carriers of merciless weapons, fearless in the face of battle.
31 Her commands were tremendous, not to be resisted.
32 Altogether she made eleven of that kind.
33 Among the gods, her sons, whom she constituted her host,
34 She exalted Qingu and magnified him among them.
35 The leadership of the army, the direction of the host,
36 The bearing of weapons, campaigning, the mobilization of conflict,
37 The chief executive power of battle supreme command,
38 She entrusted to him and set him on a throne.
39 "I have cast the spell for you and exalted you in the host of the gods,
40 I have delivered to you the rule of all the gods.
41 You are indeed exalted, my spouse, you are renowned,
42 Let your commands prevail over all the Anunnaki."
43 She gave him the tablet of Destinies and fastened it to his breast,

44 (Saying) "Your order may not he changed; let the utterance of your mouth be firm."
45 After Qingu was elevated and had acquired the power of Anuship
46 He decreed the destinies for the gods. her sons:
47 "May the utterance of your mouths subdue the fire-god,
48 May your poison by its accumulation put down aggression."

The majority of Tablets II to IV consist primarily of the political and military positionings and rhetoric of several characters. Thus the commentary of these sections will be kept to a minimum.

49 Ansar heard; the matter was profoundly disturbing.
50 He cried "Woe!" and bit his lip.
51 His heart was in fury, his mind could not be calmed.
52 Over Ea his son his cry was faltering.
53 "My son, you who provoked the war,
54 Take responsibility for whatever you alone have done!
55 You set out and killed Apsu,
56 And as for Tiamat, whom you made furious, where is her equal?"
57 The gatherer of counsel, the learned prince,
58 The creator of wisdom, the god Nudimmud
59 With soothing words and calming utterance
60 Gently answered [his] father Ansar
61 "My father, deep mind, who decrees destiny,
62 Who has the power to bring into being and destroy,
63 Ansar, deep mind, who decrees destiny,
64 Who has the power to bring into being and to destroy,

65 I want to say something to you, calm down for me for a moment
66 And consider that I performed a helpful deed.
67 Before I killed Apsu
68 Who could have seen the present situation?
69 Before I quickly made an end of him
70 What were the circumstances were I to destroy him?"
71 Ansar heard, the words pleased him.
72 His heart relaxed to speak to Ea,
73 "My son, your deeds are fitting for a god,
74 You are capable of a fierce, unequalled blow […]
75 Ea, your deeds are fitting for a god,
76 You are capable of a fierce, unequalled blow […]
77 Go before Tiamat and appease her attack,
78 […] her fury with […] incantation."
79 He heard the speech of Ansar his father,
80 He took the road to her, proceeded on the route to her.
81 He went, he perceived the tricks of Tiamat,
82 […], fell silent, and turned back.
83 […] entered the presence of august Ansar
84 Penitently addressing him,
85 […], Tiamat's deeds are too much for me.
86 I perceived her planning, and […] incantation was not equal.
87 Her strength is mighty, she is full of dread,
88 She is altogether very strong, none can go against her.
89 Her very loud cry did not diminish,
90 […] of her cry and turned back.
91 […], do not lose hope, send a second person against her.
92 Though a woman's strength is very great, it is not equal to a man's.
93 Disband her cohorts, break up her plans

94 Before she lays her hands on us."
95 Ansar cried out in intense fury,
96 Addressing Anu his son,
97 "Honoured son, hero, warrior,
98 Whose strength is mighty, whose attack is irresistible
99 Hasten and stand before Tiamat,
100 Appease her rage that her heart may relax
101 If she does not harken to your words,
102 Address to her words of petition that she may be appeased."
103 He heard the speech of Ansar his father,
104 He took the road to her, proceeded on the route to her.
105 Anu went, he perceived the tricks of Tiamat,
106 He stopped, fell silent, and turned back.
107 He entered the presence of Ansar the father who begat him,
108 Penitently addressing him.
109 "My father, Tiamat's […] are too much for me.
110 I perceived her planning, but my […] was not […]
111 Her strength is mighty, she is […] of dread,
112 She is altogether very strong, no one […]
113 Her very loud noise does not diminish,
114 I became afraid of her cry and turned back.
115 My father, do not lose hope, send another person against her.
116 Though a woman's strength is very great, it is not equal to a man's.
117 Disband her cohorts, break up her plans,
118 Before she lays her hands on us."
119 Ansar lapsed into silence, staring at the ground,
120 He nodded to Ea, shaking his head.
121 The Igigi and all the Anunnaki had assembled,
122 They sat in tight-lipped silence.

This section appears to indicate that Ansar and Ea after a lengthy debate, have resolved themselves to some specific action, perhaps utilizing the "tablet of destinies." Lines 119 to 122 describe the final moments of entering a command which gathers (or displays) the Anunnaki (constellations for the purpose of spatial orientation) and some previously unmentioned objects called the 'Igigi'. Here, with the tactical data displayed in front of Ea and Ansar, they sit in "tight-lipped silence", having said all there was to say, and knowing what action must be performed, yet still solemnly hesitant as another tense moment passes, before the final 'commit' button is selected.

Even now, they cannot bring themselves to finalize it. There is still disagreement between the two. Instead, they need to process the decision mentally and emotionally. Ansar goes off alone to ponder it. Ea though wants to discuss the matter with Marduk, whom he summons. He convinces Marduk to side with him and sends him to try to convince Ansar.

123 No god would go to face [...]
124 Would go out against Tiamat [...]
125 Yet the lord Ansar, the father of the great gods,
126 Was angry in his heart, and did not summon any one.
127 A mighty son, the avenger of his father,
128 He who hastens to war, the warrior Marduk
129 Ea summoned [...] to his private chamber
130 To explain to him his plans.
131 "Marduk, give counsel, listen to your father.
132 You are my son, who gives me pleasure,
133 Go reverently before Ansar,

134 Speak, take your stand, appease him with your glance."
135 Bel rejoiced at his father's words,
136 He drew near and stood in the presence of Ansar.
137 Ansar saw him, his heart filled with satisfaction,
138 He kissed his lips and removed his fear.
139 "My [...] do not hold your peace, but speak forth,
140 I will go and fulfil your desires!
141 [...] do not hold your peace, but speak forth,
142 I will go and fulfil your desires!
143 Which man has drawn up his battle array against you?
144 And will Tiamat, who is a woman, attack you with weapons?
145 [...], begetter, rejoice and be glad,
146 Soon you will tread on the neck of Tiamat!
147 [...], begetter, rejoice and be glad,
148 Soon you will tread on the neck of Tiamat!
149 [...] my son, conversant with all knowledge,
150 Appease Tiamat with your pure spell.
151 Drive the storm chariot without delay,
152 And with a [...] which cannot be repelled turn her back.

Line 151 draws a strong parallel with a recurring theme in the Hebrew scriptures that describe some kind of vehicle, typically airborne, that is accompanied by storm-like clouds and flashes of "lightning".[4]

---

[4] Goudsward, Ken; *UFOs In The Bible*, 2021, Dimensionfold Publishing, ISBN 978-1-989940-08-2

153 Bel rejoiced at his father's words,
154 With glad heart he addressed his father,
155 "Lord of the gods, Destiny of the great gods,
156 If I should become your avenger,
157 If I should bind Tiamat and preserve you,
158 Convene an assembly and proclaim for me an exalted destiny.
159 Sit, all of you, in Upsukkinakku with gladness,
160 And let me, with my utterance, decree destinies instead of you.
161 Whatever I instigate must not be changed,
162 Nor may my command be nullified or altered."

Tablet III

1 Ansar opened his mouth
2 And addressed Kaka, his vizier,
3 "Vizier Kaka, who gratifies my pleasure,
4 I will send you to Lahmu and Lahamu.

    Here is more evidence of our suggested interpretation of these names referring to places rather than anthropomorphic "gods". Kaka is sent somewhere to act as an attaché representing Ansar in a foreign council meeting. It seems that the decision is now out the hands of Ea and Ansu and is being escalated to a higher court.

5 You are skilled in making inquiry, learned in address.
6 Have the gods, my fathers, brought to my presence.
7 Let all the gods be brought,
8 Let them confer as they sit at table.
9 Let them eat grain, let them drink ale,
10 Let them decree the destiny for Marduk their avenger.
11 Go, be gone, Kaka, stand before them,
12 And repeat to them all that I tell you:
13 "Ansar, your son, has sent me,
14 And I am to explain his plans.

    At this point lines 15 to 52 are a repetition of Tablet II, lines 11 to 48. Again, this chunk contains the section regarding the zodiac and computer programs. Thus it is the third repetition of that section.

53 I sent Anu, but he could not face her.
54 Nudimmud took fright and retired.
55 Marduk, the sage of the gods, your son, has come forward,
56 He has determined to meet Tiamat.
57 He has spoken to me and said,

The next 7 lines are a direct quote from Tablet II, lines 156 to 162.

58 If I should become your avenger,
59 If I should bind Tiamat and preserve you,
60 Convene an assembly and proclaim for me an exalted destiny.
61 Sit, all of you, in Upsukkinakku with gladness,
62 And let me, with my utterance, decree destinies instead of you.
63 Whatever I instigate must not be changed,
64 Nor may my command be nullified or altered."

65 Quickly, now, decree your destiny for him without delay,
66 That he may go and face your powerful enemy."
67 Kaka went. He directed his steps
68 To Lahmu and Lahamu, the gods his fathers.
69 He prostrated himself, he kissed the ground before them,
70 He got up, saying to them he stood,

The next section, lines 71 to 124 (53 lines) are a direct quote from Tablet II, lines 13 to 66.

71 All the gods have turned to her,
72 Even those you begat also take her side
73 They [...] and took the side of Tiamat,
74 Fiercely plotting, unresting by night and day,
75 Lusting for battle, raging, storming,
76 They set up a host to bring about conflict.
77 Mother Hubur, who forms everything,
78 Supplied irresistible weapons, and gave birth to giant serpents.
79 They had sharp teeth, they were merciless.
80 With poison instead of blood she filled their bodies.
81 She clothed the fearful monsters with dread,
82 She loaded them with an aura and made them godlike.
83 (She said,) "Let their onlooker feebly perish,
84 May they constantly leap forward and never retire."
85 She created the Hydra, the Dragon, the Hairy Hero,
86 The Great Demon, the Savage Dog, and the Scorpion-man,
87 Fierce demons, the Fish-man, and the Bull-man,
88 Carriers of merciless weapons, fearless in the face of battle.
89 Her commands were tremendous, not to be resisted.
90 Altogether she made eleven of that kind.
91 Among the gods, her sons, whom she constituted her host,
92 She exalted Qingu and magnified him among them.
93 The leadership of the army, the direction of the host,
94 The bearing of weapons, campaigning, the mobilization of conflict,
95 The chief executive power of battle supreme command,
96 She entrusted to him and set him on a throne.

97 "I have cast the spell for you and exalted you in the host of the gods,
98 I have delivered to you the rule of all the gods.
99 You are indeed exalted, my spouse, you are renowned,
100 Let your commands prevail over all the Anunnaki."
101 She gave him the tablet of Destinies and fastened it to his breast,
102 "Your order may not he changed; let the utterance of your mouth be firm."
103 After Qingu was elevated and had acquired the power of Anuship
104 He decreed the destinies for the gods. her sons:
105 "May the utterance of your mouths subdue the fire-god,
106 May your poison by its accumulation put down aggression."
107 Ansar heard; the matter was profoundly disturbing.
108 He cried "Woe!" and bit his lip.
109 His heart was in fury, his mind could not be calmed.
110 Over Ea his son his cry was faltering.
111 "My son, you who provoked the war,
112 Take responsibility for whatever you alone have done!
113 You set out and killed Apsu,
114 And as for Tiamat, whom you made furious, where is her equal?"
115 The gatherer of counsel, the learned prince,
116 The creator of wisdom, the god Nudimmud
117 With soothing words and calming utterance
118 Gently answered [his] father Ansar
119 "My father, deep mind, who decrees destiny,
120 Who has the power to bring into being and destroy,
121 Ansar, deep mind, who decrees destiny,

122 Who has the power to bring into being and to destroy,
123 I want to say something to you, calm down for me for a moment
124 And consider that I performed a helpful deed.

125 When Lahmu and Lahamu heard, they cried aloud.
126 All the Igigi moaned in distress,
127 "What has gone wrong that she took this decision about us?
128 We did not know what Tiamat was doing."
129 All the great gods who decree destinies
130 Gathered as they went,
131 They entered the presence of Ansar and became filled with […],
132 They kissed one another as they […] in the assembly.
133 They conferred as they sat at table,
134 They ate grain, they drank ale.
135 They strained the sweet liquor through their straws,
136 As they drank beer and felt good,
137 They became quite carefree, their mood was merry,
138 And they decreed the fate for Marduk, their avenger.

Tablet IV

1 They set a lordly dais for him
2 And he took his seat before his fathers to receive kingship.
3 "You are the most honoured among the great gods,
4 Your destiny is unequalled, your command is like Anu's.
5 Marduk, you are the most honoured among the great gods,
6 Your destiny is unequalled, your command is like Anu's.
7 Henceforth your order will not be annulled,
8 It is in your power to exalt and abase.
9 Your utterance is sure, your command cannot be rebelled against,
10 None of the gods will transgress the line you draw.
11 Shrines for all the gods needs provisioning,
12 That you may be established where their sanctuaries are.
13 You are Marduk, our avenger,

Amongst the rhetoric we finally come to several interesting facts. Take note of the following lines 14 to 28.

14 We have given you kingship over the sum of the whole universe.
15 Take your seat in the assembly, let your word be exalted,
16 Let your weapons not miss the mark but may they slay your enemies.
17 Bel, spare him who trusts in you,
18 But destroy the god who set his mind on evil."

19 They set a constellation in the middle
20 And addressed Marduk, their son,
21 "Your destiny, Bel, is superior to that of all the gods,
22 Command and bring about annihilation and re-creation.
23 Let the constellation disappear at your utterance,
24 With a second command let the constellation reappear."
25 He gave the command and the constellation disappeared,
26 With a second command the constellation came into being again.
27 When the gods, his fathers, saw (the effect of) his utterance,
28 They rejoiced and offered congratulation: "Marduk is the king!"

Marduk's jurisdiction is here stated to consist of "the whole universe". In order to prove this fact, a simple display of power is demanded. This act appears to consist of the turning on and off and back on again of a voice activated display of "the constellation". It seems that Marduk is able to successfully control the computer display. He has been granted the computer access required to rule the universe.

29 They added to him a mace, a throne, and a rod,
30 They gave him an irresistible weapon that overwhelms the foe:
31 (They said,) "Go, cut Tiamat's throat,
32 And let the winds bear up her blood to give the news."
33 The gods, his fathers, decreed the destiny of Bel,

34 And set him on the road, the way of prosperity and success.

Marduk is finally granted freedom to go ahead with his plan to kill Tiamat. In so doing, he will depose her from her position as ruler. The counsel pre-emptively appoints Marduk as supreme ruler of the universe, so that he acts in authority in his quest.

35 He fashioned a bow and made it his weapon,
36 He set an arrow in place, put the bow string on.
37 He took up his club and held it in his right hand,
38 His bow and quiver he hung at his side.
39 He placed lightning before him,
40 And filled his body with tongues of flame.
41 He made a net to enmesh the entrails of Tiamat,
42 And stationed the four winds that no part of her escape.
43 The South Wind, the North Wind, the East Wind, the West Wind,
44 He put beside his net, winds given by his father, Anu.
45 He fashioned the Evil Wind, the Dust Storm, Tempest,
46 The Four-fold Wind, the Seven-fold Wind, the Chaos-spreading Wind, the […] Wind.
47 He sent out the seven winds that he had fashioned,
48 And they took their stand behind him to harass Tiamat's entrails.

Marduk's tactics here are very much those of a military manoeuvre against a collective entity. This is not the type of thing one would do when assassinating a specific person. Clearly Tiamat is a group of individuals, perhaps a city, nation, or planet. Marduk sets up a perimeter with what sounds like an automated sensor array in order to detect and destroy any fleeing vessels.

49 Bel took up the Storm-flood, his great weapon,
50 He rode the fearful chariot of the irresistible storm.
51 Four steeds he yoked to it and harnessed them to it,
52 The Destroyer, The Merciless, The Trampler, The Fleet.
53 Their lips were parted, their teeth bore venom,
54 They were strangers to weariness, trained to sweep forward.
55 At his right hand he stationed raging battle and strife,
56 On the left, conflict that overwhelms a united battle array.
57 He was clad in a tunic, a fearful coat of mail,
58 And on has head he wore an aura of terror.
59 Bel proceeded and set out on his way,
60 He set his face toward the raging Tiamat.
61 In his lips he held a spell,
62 He grasped a plant to counter poison in his hand,
63 Thereupon they milled around him, the gods milled around him,
64 The gods, his fathers, milled around him, the gods milled around him.
65 Bel drew near, surveying the maw of Tiamat,
66 He observed the tricks of Qingu, her spouse.

At this point a hitherto unknown fact is revealed to the astute reader. Whereas up until now Quingu is spoken of only by Hubur, we now see that Quingu is the spouse of none other that Tiamat herself. Therefore, Hubur is Tiamat. Thus, it was Tiamat all along who set up the zodiacal Anunnaki. Therefore, if our previous proposal is correct, that Hubur refers to the galactic plane of the Milky Way, then Tiamat also refers to the galaxy. So, the enemy of Marduk is revealed to be a central galactic authority.

When Marduk is appointed ruler of "the universe", it is perhaps more accurate to say that he is rebelling against an old, established galaxy-centric empire in favor of a newer, more universalist regime. In many ways, this is a battle of ideologies, doctrines, perceptions, and persuasion. In such a battle self-doubt plays a role, as indicated in the next section.

67 As he looked, he lost his nerve,
68 His determination went and he faltered.
69 His divine aides, who were marching at his side,
70 Saw the warrior, the foremost, and their vision became dim.
71 Tiamat cast her spell without turning her neck,
72 In her lips she held untruth and lies,
73 […]
74 In their […] they have assembled by you.
75 Bel […] the Storm-flood, his great weapon,
76 And with these words threw it at the raging Tiamat,
77 "Why are you aggressive and arrogant,
78 And strive to provoke battle?
79 The younger generation have shouted, outraging their elders,
80 But you, their mother, hold pity in contempt.
81 Qingu you have named to be your spouse,

82 And you have improperly appointed him to the rank of Anuship.
83 Against Ansar, king of the gods, you have stirred up trouble,
84 And against the gods, my fathers, your trouble is established.
85 Deploy your troops, gird on your weapons,
86 You and I will take our stand and do battle."
87 When Tiamat heard this
88 She went insane and lost her reason.
89 Tiamat cried aloud and fiercely,
90 All her lower members trembled beneath her.
91 She was reciting an incantation, kept reciting her spell,
92 While the [...] were sharpening their weapons of war.
93 Tiamat and Marduk, the sage of the gods, came together,
94 Joining in strife, drawing near to battle.
95 Bel spread out his net and enmeshed her;
96 He let loose the Evil Wind, the rear guard, in her face.
97 Tiamat opened her mouth to swallow it,
98 She let the Evil Wind in so that she could not close her lips.
99 The fierce winds weighed down her belly,
100 Her inwards were distended and she opened her mouth wide.
101 He let fly an arrow and pierced her belly,
102 He tore open her entrails and slit her inwards,
103 He bound her and extinguished her life,
104 He threw down her corpse and stood on it.
105 After he had killed Tiamat, the leader,
106 Her assembly dispersed, her host scattered.
107 Her divine aides, who went beside her,
108 In trembling and fear beat a retreat.

109 […] to save their lives,
110 But they were completely surrounded, unable to escape.
111 He bound them and broke their weapons,
112 And they lay enmeshed, sitting in a snare,
113 Hiding in corners, filled with grief,
114 Bearing his punishment, held in a prison.

Marduk delivers Tiamat's death-blow in the form of what may have been an enormous nuclear blast or some other weapon capable of exploding an planet. He takes captive many refugees, crushes any semblances of the remains of Tiamat's civilization, and takes their technologies for him self.

115 The eleven creatures who were laden with fearfulness,
116 The throng of devils who went as grooms at her right hand,
117 He put ropes upon them and bound their arms,
118 Together with their warfare he trampled them beneath him.
119 Now Qingu, who had risen to power among them,
120 He bound and reckoned with the Dead Gods.
121 He took from him the Tablet of Destinies, which was not properly his,
122 Sealed it with a seal and fastened it to his own breast.
123 After the warrior Marduk had bound and slain his enemies,
124 Had […] the arrogant enemy […]
125 Had established victory for Ansar over all his foes,
126 Had fulfilled the desire of Nudimmud,

127 He strengthened his hold on the Bound Gods,
128 And returned to Tiamat, whom he had bound.
129 Bel placed his feet on the lower parts of Tiamat
130 And with his merciless club smashed her skull.
131 He severed her arteries
132 And let the North wind bear up [...] to give the news.
133 His fathers saw it and were glad and exulted;
134 They brought gifts and presents to him.
135 Bel rested, surveying the corpse,
136 In order to divide the lump by a clever scheme.
137 He split her into two like a dried fish:
138 One half of her he set up and stretched out as the heavens.
139 He stretched the skin and appointed a watch
140 With the instruction not to let her waters escape.
141 He crossed over the heavens, surveyed the celestial parts,
142 And adjusted them to match the Apsu, Nudimmud's abode.
143 Bel measured the shape of the Apsu
144 And set up Esarra, a replica of Esgalla.
145 In Esgalla, Esarra which he had built, and the heavens,
146 He settled in their shrines Anu, Enlil, and Ea.

    The final 6 lines of Tablet IV speak of Marduk flying across "the heavens", taking measurements, adjusting his data, and setting up a simulation of some kind. It is not clear if this simulation was a physical exact replica of an object, or some kind of computer visualization or database. The fact that Marduk takes the Tablet of Destinies from Quingu suggests a technology transfer that may imply that he is simply scraping the data in order to integrate it into his own databases. Recalling line 79 of Tablet I, Marduk's primary base of operations was called the "room of archetypes". This secondary setup, then, may be an updated copy of that first base. The other name for his base was the "chamber of destinies"; in other words, it was where the predictive algorithms ran. The whole setup might have resembled some kind of virtual reality video game that he "settled in". The following tablet goes into greater detail about this setup.

Tablet V

1 He fashioned heavenly stations for the great gods,
2 And set up constellations, the patterns of the stars.
3 He appointed the year, marked off divisions,
4 And set up three stars each for the twelve months.
5 After he had organized the year,
6 He established the heavenly station of Nibiru to fix the stars' intervals.
7 That none should transgress or be slothful

As Marduk sets up his new system, it is clear that one of the main elements is a new system of constellations that differs from that of his predecessor Tiamat/Hubur. However, it is clear that he integrates Tiamat's data into his new system. In my opinion there is only one feasible way of interpreting these facts. Clearly, Marduk saw value in Tiamat's system. However, he could not simply use her existing system as is. He had to make significant adjustments and set up his own system of constellations. Why would that be the case? The answer is obvious. Tiamat's data did not work for Marduk's location. There was enough difference in the patterns of the stars between the two locations, that the system required a re-jigging using fresh data as measured from Marduk's location. That is to say that the night sky looks considerably different depending upon which planet the observer is on. This is why, as we already observed, Hubur/Tiamat's data did not match up with the order of zodiac signs that we are familiar with. Although both systems appear to use the same signs, indicating that the referred and signified object is the same in both systems, their orientation differs significantly. This point cannot be overstated. The only way that there would be any noticeable differences between navigational charts of this type, is that two observation locations are significantly far apart, on the order of astronomical distances. Simply moving to the other side of any given planet is insufficient to necessitate such adjustments. Essentially, this fact rules out our previous suggestion that these places be interpreted as cities or nations. Only by interpreting them as cosmic location points does the narrative make any sense. Marduk had taken a system designed on one planet and transported it to another planet, a move that required a re-calibration of the system with fresh data.

The text tells us that Marduk established "heavenly stations". Some may interpret this to mean physical space stations, but this is clearly not the case given the context. These heavenly stations are simply data point anchors. He marked off divisions of twelve, using the system created by Tiamat, then further divided each twelfth into "three stars each for the twelve". This can be interpreted as a further subdivision around the celestial equator, for a total of 36 "quadrants" of ten degrees each. However, an equally feasible interpretation here is that of an additional, off axis sector both below and above that equator, yielding a fully spherical grid of reference points. Sitchin calls these off-axis sections, "the way of Ea", and "the way of Enlil".[5] Marduk set up all these reference points, anchored to an additional point of reference, "to fix the stars' intervals, that none should transgress or be slothful". This primary anchor point was given the name Nibiru. The word Nibiru is an ancient Akkadian word meaning "crossing" or "point of

---

[5] Sitchin, p. 190

transition", which is often used in association with rivers, such as a ferry-boat location, for, or bridge.[6] Recalling that Hubur means river, and can apply to the Milky Way galaxy as seen from earth, it becomes clear that Nibiru is the point in the sky as seen from earth, where the milky way crosses the celestial equator. These two celestial "structures" are set at a specific angle,[7] due to the inclination of the earth's rotational axis and the inclination of the plane of the solar system's rotation known as the "ecliptic".[8] In a strictly terrestrial sense, there is no particular advantage to involving the Milky Way into zodiacal calculations. It is unnecessary for determining calendars and calculating seasons. The constellations themselves suffice for these types of uses. However, if one is to consider the more general purpose of Marduk's system, the importance of the galactic position becomes a critical point. This is because Marduk's system is not a calendrical one at all; this is merely a secondary use. The primary purpose of this system is that of tracking locations and calculating for navigation in the space beyond earth. This was a computerized navigation system for spaceships.

In 2015, the Cuneiform Digital Library Bulletin published the findings of a study[9] headed by Immanuel Freedman that analyzed the usage and nature of the concept of astronomical "crossings" within the entire extant body of cuneiform texts. The conclusion was that the cuneiform

---

[6] Akkadian Dictionary: nēbertu, nēburu

[7] Currently this angle is 23.44 degrees, but it changes slightly in a cyclic pattern that repeats over several million years.

[8] The geometries and patterns involved are actually somewhat more complex, but this simplification is correct in a general sense.

[9] Freedman, Immanuel; *The Marduk Star Nēbiru*. Cuneiform Digital Library Bulletin 2015:3

evidence supports a hypothesis that "the name Nēbiru may be assigned to any visible astronomical object that marks an equinox". A simpler way to say this is that the "crossing point" is a "spot" rather than a specific object. Since the zodiacal signs are perceived to move across our sky, the figurative parade of animals is seen to progress through this spot, across the "river" of the Milky Way. This constant motion caused by the combined effects of the earth's rotation, its revolution around the sun, and several other relatively minor factors, works against any would-be astronaut planning a space mission. The computational requirements employed by NASA and their ilk are mind-bogglingly complex. Without this level of detail space flight would be impossible. To clarify, the space flight itself would be possible, but actually arriving at the intended destination would not be. Marduk was very much aware of this fact and put much attention toward ensuring accurate data and strong algorithms.

8 He fixed the heavenly stations of Enlil and Ea with it.
9 Gates he opened on both sides,
10 And put strong bolts at the left and the right.
11 He placed the heights in her belly,

The next section refers to Nannar which is an Akkadian word for "moon". Marduk programmed lunar data into his system as well.

12 He created Nannar, entrusting to him the night.
13 He appointed him as the jewel of the night to fix the days,

14 And month by month without ceasing he elevated him with a crown,
15 (Saying,) "Shine over the land at the beginning of the month,
16 Resplendent with horns to fix six days.
17 On the seventh day the crown will be half size,
18 On the fifteenth day, halfway through each month, stand in opposition.

The next section speaks of Shamash, our sun, which Marduk also programmed in. The section appears to discuss correlations and discrepancies between Lunar and Solar calendars, however, the Tablet is damaged and many words are unintelligible.

19 When Shamash [...] you on the horizon,
20 Diminish in the proper stages and shine backwards.
21 On the 29th day, draw near to the path of Shamash,
22 [...] the 30th day, stand in conjunction and rival Shamash.
23 I have [...] the sign, follow its track,
24 Draw near [...] give judgment.
25 [...] Shamash, constrain [...] and violence,
26 [...] me.

Lines 27 to 34 of the tablet are so badly damaged as to be completely unreadable.

35 At the end [...]
36 Let there [...] the 29th day [...]

37 After [...] the decrees [...]
38 The organization of front and [...]
39 He made the day [...]
40 Let the year be equally [...]
41 At the new year [...]
42 The year [...]
43 Let there be regularly [...]
44 The projecting bolt [...]
45 After he had [...]
46 The watches of night and day [...]
47 The foam which Tiamat [...]
48 Marduk fashioned [...]
49 He gathered it together and made it into clouds.
50 The raging of the winds, violent rainstorms,
51 The billowing of mist—the accumulation of her spittle—
52 He appointed for himself and took them in his hand.

Lines 47 to 52 may refer again to the remnant survivors from Tiamat's planet. Given the position of this section of text within the data that Marduk has been adding to his database, this most likely means that he has taken a census of these survivors and is tracking them with as a group and individually with personal ID.

The following section may refer to reparations made for these survivors.

53 He put her head in position and poured out [...]
54 He opened the abyss and it was sated with water.
55 From her two eyes he let the Euphrates and Tigris flow,
56 He blocked her nostrils, but left [...]

57 He heaped up the distant […] on her breasts,
58 He bored wells to channel the springs.
59 He twisted her tail and wove it into the Durmah(u,
60 […] the Apsu beneath his feet.
61 […] her crotch—it wedged up the heavens
62 […] he stretched out and made it firm as the earth.
63 […] he had finished his work inside Tiamat,
64 […] his net and let it right out.
65 He surveyed the heavens and the earth […]
66 […] their bonds […]

    Marduk has now completed his programming and data entry. He now grants system access to his father, Ea and his grandfather Anu.

67 After he had formulated his regulations and composed […] decrees,
68 He attached guide-ropes and put them in Ea's hands.
69 [The Tablet] of Destinies which Qingu had taken and carried,
70 He took charge of it as a […] and presented it to Anu.
71 […] of battle, which he had tied on or had put on his head,
72 […] he brought before his fathers.
73 […] the eleven creatures to which Tiamat had given birth and
74 He broke their weapons and bound them to his feet.
75 He made images of them and stationed them at the […] of the Apsu,
76 To be a sign never to be forgotten.

Marduk shows Ea and Apsu the new system, and particularly, how to interpret the zodiacal signs, which he prints out for their continued reference.

He also gives a demonstration to a wider audience, all of whom celebrate his achievement. In fact, his coup now accomplished, the authorities assemble for an official recognition of Marduk's primacy and legitimacy of rule.

77 [...] saw it and were jubilantly happy,
78 [...] Lahmu, Lahamu and all his fathers.
79 Ansar [...] him and published abroad his title, "Victorious King,"
80 Anu, Enlil and Ea gave him gifts.
81 Mother Damkina, who bore him, hailed him,
82 With a clean festal robe she made his face shine.
83 To Usmu, who held her present to give the news,
84 [...] the vizierate of the Apsu and the care of the holy places.
85 The Igigi assembled and all did obeisance to him,
86 Every one of the Anunnaki was kissing his feet.

It appears that the Igigi are essentially the members of some form of parliament or senate. Their council is continuous, spanning the reign of both Tiamat and Marduk. The apparent conflation of the Igigi and Anunnaki that appears in Line 85 and 86 can be interpreted by recalling that the Anunnaki refers not to people but the constellations of the zodiac. It is useful to recall the shift of personal names to place names, for now this seems applicable to the constellations as well. A clue to this interpretation is provided in Line 83/84. Usmu is appointed as the new vizier under Marduk. Keep in mind that the Igigi are not a planetary senate. Their jurisdiction, as has already been noted, is galactic at minimum, and possibly even universal. Usmu's viziership is however local to Marduk's specific region. This is clear in Line 84's reference to the "viziership of the Apsu", the Apsu being the name of the location (whether city or palace is not clear), as established in Tablet I Line 76.

Thus, with Usmu established in the region of Apsu, we turn to the other regions. The Anunnaki represent the other regions be way of pointing in the directions of those regions. This is exactly parallel to modern shorthand of referring to "the West" and "the Arctic" or even "Asia" and the other continents as simply an easy way to refer to a large collection of individual nations, territories, or geographic areas. In space there is no East and West, bet it makes sense to refer to the direction of constellations, from the point of view of a given location where the observer is currently located. In other words, am assembly, even a virtual one, must refer to special directionality in terms that pertain to the spatial location of the conference's host. Thus, a celebration and vizieral installation centered on Marduk and Usmu in Apsu will not surprisingly welcome delegates from Taurus and Leo and Capricorn, rather than listing the possibly hundred of individual planets represented. Even this though, is onerous; one cannot mention only three of twelve, and listing even twelve separate zones become unwieldy and verbose. The obvious greeting would be "Welcome Igigi from all the constellations!" and this is precisely what we do find. The Igigi assembled from "every one of the Anunnaki."

87 They all [...] to show their submission,
88 [...] they stood, they bowed down, "Behold the king!"
89 His fathers [...] and took their fill of his beauty,
90 Bel listened to their utterance, being girded with the dust of battle.
91 [...]
92 Anointing his body with [...] cedar perfume.
93 He clothed himself in [...] lordly robe,
94 With a crown of terror as a royal aura.
95 He took up his club and held it in his right hand,
96 [...]he grasped in his left.
97 [...]
98 [...] he set his feet.
99 He put upon [...]
100 The sceptre of prosperity and success [...] at his side.
101 After [...] the aura [...]
102 He [...] his sack, the Apsu, with a fearful [...]
103 Was settled like [...]
104 In [...] throne room [...]
105 In his [...]
106 Every one of the gods [...]
107 Lahmu and Lahamu [...]
108 Opened their mouths and [...] the Igigi gods,
109 "Previously Marduk was our beloved son,
110 Now he is your king, heed his command!"
111 Next, they all spoke up together,
112 "His name is Lugaldimmerankia, trust in him!"
113 When they had given kingship to Marduk,
114 They addressed to him a benediction for prosperity and success,
115 "Henceforth you are the caretaker of our shrine,
116 Whatever you command, we will do!"

117 Marduk opened his mouth to speak
118 And addressed the gods his fathers,
119 "Above the Apsu, the emerald abode,
120 Opposite Esarra, which I built for you,
121 Beneath the celestial parts, whose floor I made firm,

A couple of uncanny parallels require a mention here, for Marduk specifically speaks of three unusual architectural features: "the emerald abode, beneath celestial parts, with a firm floor". Assuming that an "emerald abode" is made mostly of emerald (or something similar in color and other attributes) we may assume that the majority of its parts are indeed made of or at least adorned with these emerald-like materials. A golden palace is only so-named if it has *a lot* of gold. We imagine gold on walls, floors and ceilings. Thus, an emerald abode can be assumed to have an emerald floor and an emerald ceiling, particularly when one goes out of their way to bother bringing up these particular components. If only the walls were emerald, why draw our attention to the floor and ceiling?

This exact description of a blue-green gemlike floor and ceiling occurs several times within the Hebrew Bible, in the books of Exodus and Ezekiel. Oddly, these occurrences also focus very specifically on the floor and the ceiling. They both are also connected to other mysterious objects made of emerald, including at least two separate objects which bear a striking resemblance to Marduk's Tablet of Destinies. The Biblical accounts also appear to refer to possible computational and holographic display technologies similar to Marduk's simulation.[10] This brings up a possibility that Marduk's coronation may have included a virtual reality teleconferencing component.

122 I will build a house to be my luxurious abode.
123 Within it I will establish its shrine,
124 I will found my chamber and establish my kingship.
125 When you come up from the Apsu to make a decision
126 This will be your resting place before the assembly.
127 When you descend from heaven to make a decision
128 This will be your resting place before the assembly.
129 I shall call its name 'Babylon', "The Homes of the Great Gods",
130 Within it we will hold a festival: that will be the evening festival.
131 [...], his fathers, [...] this speech of his,
132 [...] they said,
133 "With regard to all that your hands have made,
134 Who has your [...]
135 With regard to the earth that your hands have made,
136 Who has your [...]
137 In Babylon, as you have named it,
138 Put our [...] for ever.
139 [...] let them our bring regular offerings
140 [...]
141 Whoever [...] our tasks which we [...]
142 Therein [...] its toil [...]

---

[10] These topics are explored in great depth in my book "UFOs In The Bible" - Goudsward, Ken; *UFOs In The Bible*, 2021, Dimensionfold Publishing, ISBN 978-1-989940-08-2

Although the text is somewhat fragmentary, Lines 133 to 142 may be interpreted as a discussion around data security wherein the Igigi query Marduk on his data security and backup policies, are suitably impressed, and subsequently ask Marduk to onboard them onto his cloud services.

143 [...]
144 They rejoiced [...]
145 The gods [...]
146 He who knows [...] them
147 He opened [...] them light,
148 [...] his speech [...]
149 He made wide [...] them [...]
150 And [...]
151 The gods bowed down, speaking to him,
152 They addressed Lugaldimmerankia, their lord,
153 "Formerly, lord, [...] son,
154 Now you are our king [...]
155 He who [...] preserved [...]
156 [...] the aura of club and sceptre.
157 Let him conceive plans [...]
158 [...] we [...]

Tablet VI

1 When Marduk heard the gods' speech
2 He conceived a desire to accomplish clever things.

    Marduk is the quintessential engineer. He has a lot of ideas, and when he sees a marketable opportunity, he already has a backlog of relevant ideas from which to draw upon. Upon the heels of the successful contracts with the Igigi, he proceeds to speak with his confidants in private about his next big idea.

3 He opened his mouth addressing Ea,
4 He counsels that which he had pondered in his heart,
5 "I will bring together blood to form bone,
6 I will bring into being Lullu, whose name shall be 'man'.
7 I will create Lullu—man
8 On whom the toil of the gods will be laid that they may rest.
9 I will skilfully alter the organization of the gods:
10 Though they are honoured as one, they shall be divided into two."
11 Ea answered, as he addressed a word to him,
12 Expressing his comments on the resting of the gods,
13 "Let one brother of theirs be given up.
14 Let him perish that people may be fashioned.
15 Let the great gods assemble
16 And let the guilty one be given up that they may be confirmed."

Marduk's new project involves bio-engineering. Marduk's skills as a computer programmer give him some fresh insights into what couple possibly be accomplished using the extant biological coding tools of DNA, RNA and other such assets. Marduk presumably already knows enough biology to know that his ideas are attainable. He must have studied these things thoroughly in his past. And he had good reason to. It was in his blood – literally. Remember the initial description of Marduk at his birth. He had four ears and four eyes, and his stature was of unusual size. He was a freak, to be perfectly blunt. He must have wondered why he looked different from everyone else. He was also "the wisest of the wise, the sage of the gods" and "he was mighty from the beginning."

One has to wonder if Marduk himself was the result of some kind of DNA manipulation. "Anu, his father's begetter, saw him, he exulted and smiled; his heart filled with joy. Anu rendered him perfect: his divinity was remarkable."

Had Ea and Damkina subjected themselves and their progeny to some kind of experimentation at the design and behest of Anu? It seems entirely possible that Anu had invented some kind of genetic engineering technologies and techniques that his superintelligent grandson Marduk was able to build upon, refine, and perfect. Quite likely, they worked together on these projects and experiments over the course of many years. Now, finally, it is ready for an unveiling.

17 Marduk assembled the great gods,
18 Using gracious direction as he gave his order,
19 As he spoke the gods heeded him:
20 The king addressed a word to the Anunnaki,
21 "Your former oath was true indeed,
22 [...] tell me the solemn truth:
23 Who is the one who instigated warfare,
24 Who made Tiamat rebel, and set battle in motion?
25 Let him who instigated warfare be given up
26 That I may lay his punishment on him; but you sit and rest.
27 The Igigi, the great gods, answered him,
28 That is, Lugaldimmerankia, the counsellor of the gods, the lord,
29 "Qingu is the one who instigated warfare,
30 Who made Tiamat rebel and set battle in motion."
31 They bound him, holding him before Ea,
32 They inflicted the penalty on him and severed his blood-vessels.

    Having attained a suitable subject among the Igigi in the form of Quingu, the project may now proceed.

33 From his blood he created mankind,
34 On whom he imposed the service of the gods, and set the gods free.
35 After the wise Ea had created mankind
36 And had imposed the service of the gods upon them—
37 That task is beyond comprehension

38 For Nudimmud performed the creation with the skill of Marduk

We now find that this bioengineering project involves not only Marduk and his grandfather Anu, but also his father Ea and uncle Nudimmud as well. This biotech firm is truly a family business, and all four men are now revealed to be skilled scientists. Their task is admitted by the author to be "beyond comprehension." They use proprietary company secrets in their corporate lab in order to create a new species. This species would be sold to their clients as workers. This species they called "man".

Next, it appears that the company goes on a hiring spree, recruiting many if not all of the Igigi into their ranks to act primarily as a security detail for the company. No doubt, now that the product had gone public, the shrewd bosses knew to expect corporate raiders.

39 King Marduk divided the gods,
40 All the Anunnaki into upper and lower groups.
41 He assigned 300 in the heavens to guard the decrees of Anu
42 And appointed them as a guard.
43 Next he arranged the organization of the netherworld.
44 In heaven and netherworld he stationed 600 gods.

The terms 'heaven' and 'netherworld' here should be read in the context with which the story thus far has taken place. On earth and other planets, and in the interstellar space between planetary systems.¹¹ Thus, the netherworld (literally 'lower world') is the planetary surface, and the heavens in this case would refer to planetary orbit, but may possibly also include patrols throughout the solar system.

45 After he had arranged all the decrees,
46 And had distributed incomes among the Anunnaki of heaven and netherworld,
47 The Anunnaki opened their mouths
48 And addressed their lord Marduk,
49 "Now, lord, seeing you have established our freedom
50 What favour can we do for you?

The Igigi receive payment in monetary form, possibly both salaries and dividends. They also receive payment in kind, with ownership of their own humans to work for them. This affords them a level of newfound freedom for which they are grateful to Marduk as CEO.

51 Let us make a shrine of great renown:
52 Your chamber will be our resting place wherein we may repose.
53 Let us erect a shrine to house a pedestal
54 Wherein we may repose when we finish."

---

[11] The interstellar scale is evidenced by the necessity to refit the zodiac, the references to the widespread nature of the Igigi, and the seemingly pan-galactic minimal size of the empire, as discussed earlier.

55 When Marduk heard this,
56 He beamed as brightly as the light of day,
57 "Build Babylon, the task you have sought.
58 Let bricks for it be moulded, and raise the shrine!"
59 The Anunnaki wielded the pick.
60 For one year they made the needed bricks.
61 When the second year arrived,
62 They raised the peak of Esagil, a replica of the Apsu.
63 They built the lofty temple tower of the Apsu
64 And for Anu, Enlil, and Ea they established its . . as a dwelling.

The Igigi now create a physical structure made of bricks. This structure is modelled after the Apsu in which Ea lives. This indicates that Ea's Apsu was not physical, otherwise what is the purpose of building a second identical structure? Therefore, our earlier suspicions are confirmed. The Apsu that Ea created was indeed a virtual reality environment in which he "lived".

65 He sat in splendour before them,
66 Surveying its horns, which were level with the base of Esarra.
67 After they had completed the work on Esagil
68 All the Anunnaki constructed their own shrines.
69 300 Igigi of heaven and 600 of the Apsu, all of them, had assembled.

Most likely the word 'shrine' here should be replaced with 'house'. All 900 of the company employees are now building residences in Babylon. The job of security guard is not one that can be readily accomplished via telework. Although the text is not explicit in this regard it is probably safe to assume that the actual people doing the making and stacking of bricks were not the literal Igigi themselves, but their new humans who were to "lighten their loads". If not physical labour, one is hard pressed to think of what other loads these humans may have been able to accomplish on behalf of their owners.

70 Bel seated the gods, his fathers, at the banquet
71 In the lofty shrine which they had built for his dwelling,
72 "This is Babylon, your fixed dwelling,
73 Take your pleasure here! Sit down in joy!

    The turn of phrase here though, gives one pause. Marduk now points out to the Igigi that Babylon is a "fixed", i.e. physical dwelling. He seems to allude to the fact that the Igigi had not previously had physical dwellings. Does this imply that all the Igigi's normal life up to now had been spent in a virtual world? If so, perhaps the humans were not built for physical labour at all, but rather, they were designed to take on computational tasks within the virtual world of the Igigi. This certainly makes sense, given that Marduk's previous products were software programs. Could it be true that humans were designed to be self replicating artificial intelligence bots intended to assist with some previously established onerous software tasks?

    This may be the case. It would certainly explain the great pleasure that the Igigi found in building with bricks and sitting down for a beer. This might be the first time they have "escaped the matrix" and experienced physical reality.

74 The great gods sat down,
75 Beer-mugs were set out and they sat at the banquet.
76 After they had enjoyed themselves inside
77 They held a service in awesome Esagil.
78 The regulations and all the rules were confirmed:
79 All the gods divided the stations of heaven and netherworld.
80 The college of the Fifty great gods took their seats,
81 The Seven gods of destinies were appointed to give decisions.
82 Bel received his weapon, the bow, and laid it before them:
83 His divine fathers saw the net which he had made.
84 His fathers saw how skilfully wrought was the structure of the bow
85 As they praised what he had made.
86 Anu lifted it up in the divine assembly,
87 He kissed the bow, saying, "It is my daughter!"
88 Thus he called the names of the bow:
89 "Long Stick" was the first; the second was, "May it hit the mark."
90 With the third name, "Bow Star", he made it to shine in the sky,
91 He fixed its heavenly position along with its divine brothers.
92 After Anu had decreed the destiny of the bow,
93 He set down a royal throne, a lofty one even for a god,
94 Anu set it there in the assembly of the gods.
95 The great gods assembled,
96 They exalted the destiny of Marduk and did obeisance.

97 They invoked a curse on themselves
98 And took an oath with water and oil, and put their hands to their throats.
99 They granted him the right to exercise kingship over the gods,
100 They confirmed him as lord of the gods of heaven and netherworld.
101 Ansar gave him his exalted name, Asalluhi
102 "At the mention of his name, let us show submission!
103 When he speaks, let the gods heed him,
104 Let his command be superior in upper and lower regions.
105 May the son, our avenger, be exalted,
106 Let his lordship be superior and himself without rival.
107 Let him shepherd the black-heads, his creatures,
108 Let them tell of his character to future days without forgetting.
109 Let him establish lavish food offerings for his fathers,
110 Let him provide for their maintenance and be caretaker of their sanctuaries,
111 Let him burn incense to rejoice their sanctums.

The following Line is vitally important.

112 Let him do on earth the same as he has done in heaven:

This is further evidence of the virtual-physical duality at play. Marduk has dominated the social, political, and business structure within the virtual world. Now he enables a new world to emerge, a physical one. It emerges complete with all the existing social, political, economic, and corporate structures of the Igigi. It comes to earth, bursting forth as a complete mature civilization. Earth goes from barren wasteland, to home of a civilized city essentially overnight.

Furthermore, this Line seems to be the first occurrence of a long recurring theme throughout human history. May Marduk not be forgotten. Nor the Igigi, for it was one of their number who coined the phrase:

"As above, so below."

And "on earth as it is in heaven"

113 Let him appoint the black-heads to worship him.
114 The subject humans should take note and call on their gods,
115 Since he commands they should heed their goddesses,
116 Let food offerings be brought […] their gods and goddesses,
117 May […] not be forgotten, may they remember their gods,
118 May they […]
119 Though the black-heads worship some one, some another god,
120 He is the god of each and every one of us!
121 Come, let us call the fifty names
122 Of him whose character is resplendent, whose achievement is the same.

The remainder of the text is a long list of praises and epithets of Marduk.

123 Marduk! As he was named by his father Anu from his birth,
124 Who supplies pasturage and watering, making the stables flourish.
125 Who bound the boastful with his weapon, the storm flood,
126 And saved the gods, his fathers, from distress.
127 He is the son, the sun-god of the gods, he is dazzling,
128 Let them ever walk in his bright light.
129 On the peoples that he created, the living beings,
130 He imposed the service of the gods and they took rest.
131 Creation and annihilation, forgiveness and exacting the penalty
132 Occur at his command, so let them fix their eyes on him.
133 Marukka: he is the god who created them
134 Who put the Anunnaki at ease, the Igigi at rest.
135 Marutukku: he is the support of land, city, and its peoples,
136 Henceforth let the peoples ever heed him.
137 Mersakusu: fierce yet deliberating, angry yet relenting,
138 His mind is wide, his heart is all-embracing.
139 Lugaldimmerankia is the name by which we all called him,
140 Whose command we have exalted above that of the gods his fathers.
141 He is the lord of all the gods of heaven and netherworld,

142 The king at whose injunctions the gods in upper and lower regions shudder.
143 Narilugaldimmerankia is the name we gave him, the mentor of every god,
144 Who established our dwellings in heaven and netherworld in time of trouble,
145 Who distributed the heavenly stations between Igigi and Anunnaki,
146 Let the gods tremble at his name and quake on their seats.
147 Asalluhi is the name by which his father Anu called him,
148 He is the light of the gods, a mighty hero,
149 Who, as his name says, is a protecting angel for god and land,
150 Who by a terrible combat saved our dwelling in time of trouble.
151 Asalluhi-Namtilla they called him secondly, the life-giving god,
152 Who, in accordance with the form [...] restored all the ruined gods,
153 The lord, who brought to life the dead gods by his pure incantation,
154 Let us praise him as the destroyer of the crooked enemies.
155 Asalluhi-Namru, as his name is called thirdly,
156 The pure god, who cleanses our character."
157 Ansar, Lahmu, and Lahamu called him by three of his names,
158 Then they addressed the gods, their sons,
159 "We have each called him by three of his names,
160 Now you call his names, like us."
161 The gods rejoiced as they heard their speech,

162 In Upsuukkinaki they held a conference,
163 "Of the warrior son, our avenger,
164 Of the provisioner, let us extol the name."
165 They sat down in their assembly, summoning the destinies,
166 And with all due rites they called his name:

Tablet VII

1 Asarre, the giver of arable land who established ploughland,
2 The creator of barley and flax, who made plant life grow.
3 Asaralim, who is revered in the counsel chamber, whose counsel excels,
4 The gods heed it and grasp fear of him.
5 Asaralimnunna, the noble, the light of the father, his begetter,
6 Who directs the decrees of Anu, Enlil, and Ea, that is Ninsiku.
7 He is their provisioner, who assigns their incomes,
8 Whose turban multiplies abundance for the land.
9 Tutu is he, who accomplishes their renovation,
10 Let him purify their sanctuaries that they may repose.
11 Let him fashion an incantation that the gods may rest,
12 Though they rise up in fury, let them withdraw.
13 He is indeed exalted in the assembly of the gods, his [...],
14 No one among the gods can [...] him.
15 (14) Tutu-Ziukkinna, the life of [...] host,
16 Who established, the pure heavens for the gods,
17 Who took charge of their courses, who appointed [...],
16 May he not be forgotten among mortals, but [...] his deeds.
19 Tutu-Ziku they called him thirdly, the establisher of purification,
20 The god of the pleasant breeze, lord of success and obedience,
21 Who produces bounty and wealth, who establishes abundance,

22 Who turns everything scant that we have into profusion,
23 Whose pleasant breeze we sniffed in time of terrible trouble,
24 Let men command that his praises be constantly uttered, let them offer worship to him.
25 As Tutu-Agaku, fourthly, let humans extol him,
26 Lord of the pure incantation, who brought the dead back to life,
27 Who showed mercy on the Bound Gods,
28 Who threw the imposed yoke on the gods, his enemies,
29 And to spare them created mankind.
30 The merciful, in whose power it is to restore to life,
31 Let his words be sure and not forgotten
32 From the mouths of the black-heads, his creatures.
33 As Tutu-Tuku, fifthly, let their mouth give expression to his pure spell,
34 Who extirpated all the wicked by his pure incantation.
35 Sazu, who knew the heart of the gods, who saw the reins,
36 Who did not let an evil-doer escape from him,
37 Who established the assembly of the gods, who rejoiced their hearts,
38 Who subjugated the disobedient, he is the gods' encompassing protection.
39 He made truth to prosper, he uprooted perverse speech,
40 He separated falsehood from truth.
41 As Sazu-Zisi, secondly, let them continually praise him, the subduer of aggressors,
42 Who ousted consternation of from the bodies of the gods, his fathers.
43 As Sazu-Suh(rim, thirdly, who extirpated every foe with

his weapons,
44 Who confounded their plans and turned them into wind.
45 He snuffed out all the wicked who came against him,
46 Let the gods ever shout acclamations in the assembly.
47 Sazu-Suhgurim, fourthly, who established success for the gods, his fathers,
48 Who extirpated foes and destroyed their offspring,
49 Who scattered their achievements, leaving no part of them,
50 Let his name be spoken and proclaimed in the land.
51 As Sazu-Zahrim, fifthly, let future generations discuss him,
52 The destroyer of every rebel, of all the disobedient,
53 Who brought all the fugitive gods into the shrines,
54 Let this name of his be established.
55 As Sazu-Zahgurim, sixthly, let them altogether and everywhere worship him,
56 Who himself destroyed all the foes in battle.
57 Enbilulu is he, the lord who supplies them abundantly,
58 Their great chosen one, who provides cereal offerings,
59 Who keeps pasturage and watering in good condition and established it for the land,
60 Who opened watercourses and distributed plentiful water.
61 Enbilulu-Epadun, lord of common land and [...]
62 Canal supervisor of heaven and netherworld, who sets the furrow,
Who establishes clean arable land in the open country,
63 Who directs irrigation ditch and canal, and marks out the furrow.
64 As Enbilulu-Gugal, canal supervisor of the water courses of the gods, let them praise him thirdly,

65 Lord of abundance, profusion, and huge stores
66 Who provides bounty, who enriches human habitations,
67 Who gives wheat, and brings grain into being.
68 Enbilulu-Hegal, who accumulates abundance for the peoples
69 Who rains down riches on the broad earth, and supplies abundant vegetation.
70 Sirsir, who heaped up a mountain on top of Tiamat,
71 Who plundered the corpse of Tiamat with [...] weapons,
72 The guardian of the land, their trustworthy shepherd,
73 Whose hair is a growing crop, whose turban is a furrow,
74 Who kept crossing the broad Sea in his fury,
75 And kept crossing over the place of her battle as though it were a bridge.
76 Sirsir-Malah they named him secondly—so be it
77 Tiamat was his boat, he was her sailor.
78 Gil, who ever heaps up piles of barley, massive mounds,
79 The creator of grain and flocks, who gives seed for the land.
80 Gilima, who made the bond of the gods firm, who created stability,
81 A snare that overwhelmed them, who yet extended favours.
82 Agilima, the lofty, who snatches off the crown, who takes charge of snow,
83 Who created the earth on the water and made firm the height of heaven.
84 Zulum, who assigns meadows for the gods and divides up what he has created,

85 Who gives incomes and food-offerings, who administers shrines.
86 Mummu, creator of heaven end underworld, who protects refugees,
87 The god who purifies heaven and underworld, secondly Zulummu,
88 In respect of whose strength none other among the gods can equal him.
89 Gišnumunab, creator of all the peoples, who made the world regions,
90 Who destroyed Tiamat's gods, and made peoples from part of them.
91 Lugalabdubur, the king who scattered the works of Tiamat, who uprooted her weapons,
92 Whose foundation is secure on the "Fore and Aft".
93 Pagalguenna, foremost of all lords, whose strength is exalted,
94 Who is the greatest among the gods, his brothers, the most noble of them all.
95 Lugaldurmah, king of the bond of the gods, lord of Durmahu,
96 Who is the greatest in the royal abode, infinitely more lofty than the other gods.
97 Aranunna, counsellor of Ea, creator of the gods, his fathers,
98 Whom no god can equal in respect of his lordly walk.
99 Dumuduku, who renews for himself his pure abode in Duku,
100 Dumuduku, without whom Lugalduku does not make a decision.
101 Lugalsuanna, the king whose strength is exalted among the gods,
102 The lord, the strength of Anu, he who is supreme,

chosen of Ansar.
103 Irugga, who plundered them all in the Sea,
104 Who grasps all wisdom, is comprehensive in understanding.
105 Irqingu, who plundered Qingu in . . . battle,
106 Who directs all decrees and establishes lordship.
107 Kinma, the director of all the gods, who gives counsel,
108 At whose name the gods bend down in reverence as before a hurricane.
109 Dingir-Esiskur—let him take his lofty seat in the House of Benediction,
110 Let the gods bring their presents before him
111 Until he receives their offerings.
112 No one but he accomplishes clever things
113 The four [...] of black-heads are his creation,
114 Apart from him no god knows the measure of their days.
115 Girru, who makes weapons [...]
116 Who accomplished clever things in the battle with Tiamat,
117 Comprehensive in wisdom, skilled in understanding,
118 A deep mind, that all the gods combined do not understand.
119 Let Addu be his name, let him cover the whole span of heaven,
120 Let him thunder with his pleasant voice upon the earth,
121 May the rumble [...] the clouds.
And give sustenance to the peoples below.
122 Asaru, who, as his name says, mustered the Divine Fates
123 He indeed is the warden of absolutely all peoples.

124 As Nibiru let him hold the crossing place of heaven and underworld,
125 They should not cross above or below, but should wait for him.
126 Nibiru is his star, which he caused to shine in the sky,
127 Let him take his stand on the heavenly staircase that they may look at him.
128 Yes, he who constantly crosses the Sea without resting,
129 Let his name be Nibiru, who grasps her middle,
130 Let him fix the paths of the stars of heaven,
131 Let him shepherd all the gods like sheep,
132 Let him bind Tiamat and put her life in mortal danger,
133 To generations yet unborn, to distant future days,
134 May he continue unchecked, may he persist into eternity.
135 Since he created the heavens and fashioned the earth,
136 Enlil, the father, called him by his own name, 'Lord of the Lands'.
137 Ea heard the names which all the Igigi called
138 And his spirit became radiant.
139 "Why! He whose name was extolled by his fathers
140 Let him, like me, be called 'Ea'.
141 Let him control the sum of all my rites,
142 Let him administer all my decrees."
143 With the word "Fifty" the great gods
144 Called his fifty names and assigned him an outstanding position.
145 They should be remembered; a leading figure should expound them,
146 The wise and learned should confer about them,
147 A father should repeat them and teach them to his son,
148 One should explain them to shepherd and herdsman.

149 If one is not negligent to Marduk, the Enlil of the gods,
150 May one's land flourish, and oneself prosper,
151 His word is reliable, his command unchanged,
152 No god can alter the utterance of his mouth.
153 When he looks in fury, he does not relent,
154 When his anger is ablaze, no god can face him.
155 His mind is deep, his spirit is all-embracing,
156 Before whom sin and transgression are sought out.
157 Instruction which a leading figure repeated before him
158 He wrote it down and stored it so that generations to come might hear it.
159 Marduk, who created the Igigi gods,
160 Though they diminish […] let them call on his name.
161 . . . the song of Marduk,
162 Who defeated Tiamat and took kingship

Line 159 makes a strange claim – "Marduk created the Igigi gods". We know this to be incorrect, since the Igigi appear in the story, and clearly existed before Marduk's birth. However, this phrase does make sense in a way, when considered with the idea that Marduk allowed the Igigi to essentially "become" physical and embody a physical existence that they had previously not experienced.

The following line contains the phrase "though they diminish", referring to the Igigi. Again, this line only makes any sense considering Marduk's freeing the Igigi from their virtual "prison". They can certainly be seen as having been diminished. They are now mortal. They are now essentially security guards, where previously they were senators. They will now further diminish in that they will physically experience sickness, pain, and growing old. However, this seems to be a price worth paying, and this line also implies that Marduk will offer some type of assistance in these types of situation if the Igigi "call on his name". It's not difficult to imagine Marduk offering all kinds of medical treatment. After all, he is the CEO of the universe's most successful biotech company.

Narrative Summary

Tablet I opens by summarizing a state before earth was populated. Apsu and Tiamat are named as individuals, although we later see Tiamat presented as a planet representative of a central governing body. A dynastic genealogy is given, for context in which a rebellion begins to fester. After some deliberation, Apsu decides that the rebels must be destroyed.

Ea, a high-ranking executive of the virtual reality hosting company utilized by the governing body, notices warning flags in his data surveillance routines which flag Apsu's plans, and he immediately takes action against Apsu. Ea locks Apsu and his partners out of their accounts, steals their data and takes over Apsu's profile, and in either a figurative or literal sense, "kills" Apsu. Some time later, the biotech branch of Ea's company makes a revolutionary leap in custom DNA modification, as exemplified by the birth of Ea's son Marduk, "the wisest of the wise".

Amidst an escalated technology race, Tiamat develops a computerized navigational system and database, centered on her planet's relatively central galactic position. The basis of Tiamat's system will later come to be known as the zodiac, whose constellations serve to divide space into regions. Tiamat did not use the word 'zodiac', and the text does not give a clear name for her system, but functionally, the two systems are equivalent.

Tensions escalate and factions grow, threatening to lead to a full-scale civil war. The matter is escalated to the galactic senate, the 'Igigi', where Ea and his executive team successfully gain majority backing. His company is already building a prototype of their own copycat version of Tiamat's navigational system. Their name for the cartographic sectioning constellations is the 'Anunnaki' – a combination of the words "An" meaning 'sky', and 'ki' indicating the earth. Hence, the Anunnaki, is simply the "earth-sky" or the view of the sky from the vantage point of earth.

Much debate occurs within and without of the Igigi senate, until finally Marduk is commissioned to destroy Tiamat and outfitted with a heavily armed fleet. Contingent on the success of his mission, Marduk is to be declared king of the entire universe.

Marduk's fleet surrounds Tiamat, blows up the planet, and captures any associated orbiting ships, but before completely annihilating the planet, Marduk manages to infiltrate Tiamat's system and copy her databases. Marduk integrates the stolen data into his Anunnaki system and adds an important new feature: a new data point named 'Nibiru' which expands the system from its planet-centric design into a new model which incorporates both local planetary equatorial perspective data and broader galactic-scale locations. Marduk's upgrades enable the system to be recalibrated around any arbitrary central point. This enables him to expand both his own operations, and indeed civilization as a whole, into hitherto unexplored reaches of the galaxy, including a hospitable but unoccupied planet which would eventually become known as Earth.

Marduk sets up a colony on Earth, recalibrating his system with terrestrial orbital features whose descriptions will later lead to our own lunar and solar calendars. The Igigi officially recognize Marduk's success in battle and he is appointed "Victorious King" of the universe. This occasion is the basis for the large quantity of acclamatory lines within the text.

Marduk, ever the shrewd businessman, leverages his soaring popularity into a strategic hiring spree and a new product line. He recruits many of the Igigi to come work for him on his new Earth base, enticing many with free biotech products. Marduk's new top-selling must-have product was none other than... Humans.

In Marduk's own words, *"I will bring into being Lullu, whose name shall be 'man'. I will create Lullu—man on whom the toil of the gods will be laid that they may rest."*

Conclusion

The Enuma Elish is a creation story. It tells of the creation of man and of the arrival of civilization to earth. But, the Enuma Elish is decidedly not a "creation myth". It is not a story of divine superbeings. It is not a story of mythical supernatural gods. It is a story of space exploration and politics, and computer engineering, and biotech. It is a story of power and greed and megalomania. It is a story of family business and family drama. It is a story of genius and normalcy, of great strength and hideous flaws. It is a story of the vastly cyclical nature of history – of progress and of lunacy, and of ultimate amnesiac technological loss.

About the Author

Ken Goudsward is a systems analyst with expertise in industrial robotics, software engineering, and data design. He enjoys applying these skills to ancient Hebrew and Sumerian documents, and the UFO phenomenon.

Other Books by Ken Goudsward:
- Fermi's Paradox Is Bullshit
- Before Roswell (with Barbara De Long)
- UFOs In The Bible
- Magic In The Bible
- The Atrahasis Epic

Novels by Ken Goudsward:
- Symphony Of Destruction (Hard Sci-Fi)
- Munchausen By Proxy For Fun And Profit (Crime/Dark Comedy)

Printed in France by Amazon
Brétigny-sur-Orge, FR